THE EXIT FOR MILLIONS BLUEPRINT™

Revealed: The Fatal Flaws That Will Kill Your Dream Of Selling Your Business For Millions

BY NICK BRADLEY

HIGH VALUE EXIT

FIELDING HOUSE PRESS UK

Published by Fielding House Press UK
Wansford, United Kingdom

The information provided in this book is for informational purposes only and is not intended to be a source of advice or credit analysis with respect to the material presented. The information and/or documents contained in this book do not constitute legal or financial advice and should never be used without first consulting with a financial professional to determine what may be best for your individual needs.

The publisher and the author do not make any guarantee or other promise as to any results that may be obtained from using the content of this book. You should never make any investment decision without first consulting with your own financial advisor and conducting your own research and due diligence. To the maximum extent permitted by law, the publisher and the author disclaim any and all liability in the event any information, commentary, analysis, opinions, advice and/or recommendations contained in this book prove to be inaccurate, incomplete or unreliable, or result in any investment or other losses.

Content contained or made available through this book is not intended to and does not constitute legal advice or investment advice and no attorney-client relationship is formed. The publisher and the author are providing this book and its contents on an "as is" basis. Your use of the information in this book is at your own risk.

For information about special discounts for bulk purchases or author interviews, appearances, and speaking engagements please scan this QR code to contact us:

First Edition

ISBN softcover: 978-1-0682439-4-3

MANY FOUNDERS AND BUSINESS OWNERS DREAM OF BUILDING A HIGH VALUE BUSINESS, GIVING THEMSELVES THE OPTION FOR A SUBSTANTIAL EXIT WHEN THE TIME COMES.

This dream outcome would undoubtedly give them the freedom they desire to secure their financial future, pursue their passions, and prioritize their family.

However, few founders ever build companies genuinely positioned for a lucrative acquisition. The sad reality is... *96% of all business owners* struggle with at least one of the following 15 reasons why sophisticated investors & Private Equity (PE) firms routinely reject deals.

With over 15+ years of experience working in PE, I became very familiar with the particular criteria that sophisticated investors use when evaluating businesses for acquisition. In fact, it was my job to assess businesses against this criteria before closing a deal.

When you get these criteria right, and meet their standards, deals with 8-figure-plus price tags and favorable terms await.

When you get these criteria wrong, and fall short in key areas, these sophisticated investors will pass on your business without hesitation.

In this guide, you will find the **Top 15 Reasons** why sophisticated investors & PE firms will NOT acquire your business, and some tips on how you can fix each of them.

AND AS YOU GO THROUGH THIS BLUEPRINT, I WANT YOU TO GIVE YOURSELF A SCORE OF RED, AMBER, OR GREEN FOR EACH REASON:

KEEP SCORE

Red: This statement represents a real problem for us that we need help solving.

Amber: There is some truth to this statement; things are okay but could use tweaking.

Green: This statement does not explain my situation; this area is a strength for us, and already working amazing.

Alright, you ready? Let's go ahead and jump in with revealing the fatal flaws that will kill your dream of selling your business for Millions (*and what you can do about it*).

1 YOUR BUSINESS IS GENERATING LOW PROFIT OR MINIMAL GROWTH.

WHAT THIS MEANS

Your business lacks profitability currently and cannot present a credible strategy for growth at scale over time. Sophisticated investors want to see financial viability today, and the potential to perpetuate earnings over time, so their investment will not only pay off but increase in value.

WHY IT MATTERS

No profit = no viability. No growth = no future value to capitalize on. Sophisticated investors heavily rely on acquiring your future earnings, not just a snapshot of past performance. In fact, past performance is only really used to build confidence in the go-forward plan.

WHAT YOU CAN DO ABOUT IT

- Achieve consistent profitability month-over-month, year-over-year. (*Especially the last trailing 12 months.*)
- Model scalable growth strategies and incorporate these into your plan.
- Recruit, train, and incentivize the right team, and build the right processes, to drive predictable growth.

SELF ASSESSMENT

My business is currently unprofitable, or low profit … and/or I lack a plan to drive predictable, scalable growth in the future.

☐ **RED**

This statement represents a real problem for us that we need help solving.

☐ **AMBER**

There is some truth to this statement; things are okay but could use tweaking.

☐ **GREEN**

This statement does not explain my situation; this area is a strength for us, and already working amazing.

2 YOUR BRAND OR OFFERING IS COMMODITIZED.

WHAT THIS MEANS

You compete in a market with lots of undifferentiated competitors, and you are not doing a sufficient job of differentiating your offer and standing out amongst the competition. When this happens, you often force yourself to compete on price rather than value. This invariably becomes a 'race to the bottom' and can kill a business quickly if not addressed.

WHY IT MATTERS

Commoditization makes it hard to compete short term and degrades value long term. You need uniqueness and differentiation to command premium pricing based on a superior product, experience or brand proposition.

WHAT YOU CAN DO ABOUT IT

- Identify brand differentiation points in line with what your market values.
- Sharpen positioning around uniqueness and remarkability, so you stand out. (*BONUS: Read Seth Godin's brilliant book "Purple Cow".*)
- Invest in research, innovation and IP protection. Your IP is one of your most valuable assets.

SELF ASSESSMENT

My brand, value proposition and overall offering lacks differentiation in my market and vs. my competitors.

☐ RED

This statement represents a real problem for us that we need help solving.

☐ AMBER

There is some truth to this statement; things are okay but could use tweaking.

☐ GREEN

This statement does not explain my situation; this area is a strength for us, and already working amazing.

3 YOUR LEADERSHIP TEAM IS EITHER NON EXISTENT OR HAS GAPS IN KEY FUNCTIONAL AREAS.

WHAT THIS MEANS

An effective, scalable business is run by a team of people and is not overly reliant on any one person. Furthermore, this team should complement each other from a skills, experience and behaviors standpoint.

WHY IT MATTERS

Sophisticated buyers want to acquire a business that has the building blocks in place to scale. The area that they will assess rigorously is the quality of the leadership team. A great team increases value, while a poor or non-existent team presents risk.

WHAT YOU CAN DO ABOUT IT

- Design your organization intentionally from the top down.
- Assess your current leaders to identify gaps.
- Don't be afraid to make changes if these are necessary. *(It is much better to 'hire fast but fire faster' ... as toleratingpoor performance will create bigger issues in the future if left unchecked.)*

SELF ASSESSMENT

My leadership team is not as effective as it could be in running day-to-day business operations and/or driving the strategy.

☐ RED

This statement represents a real problem for us that we need help solving.

☐ AMBER

There is some truth to this statement; things are okay but could use tweaking.

☐ GREEN

This statement does not explain my situation; this area is a strength for us, and already working amazing.

4 YOU HAVE TALENT GAPS ACROSS YOUR ORGANIZATION.

WHAT THIS MEANS

Certain supporting roles below the executive team require experienced leaders to drive your strategy and business model. Missing capabilities in these key roles indicates vulnerability and risk.

WHY IT MATTERS

Certain specialists become essential, particularly as you scale, as they make your business work effectively. These can be across all areas but particular consideration should be made to sales, marketing, and operations. The key thing is ... you can't scale from poor foundations, and having a strong foundation means relying on having the right people in the right seats, at all levels of your organization.

WHAT YOU CAN DO ABOUT IT

- Assess capabilities below leadership level, and across and through your organization.
- Identify critical specialists (beyond executives) that are driving your business strategy.
- Ensure your organization design is suitably balanced vs. being overly 'top heavy'.

SELF ASSESSMENT

My business has talent gaps, crucial to driving our strategy, below the leadership level, that need to be addressed.

☐ RED

This statement represents a real problem for us that we need help solving.

☐ AMBER

There is some truth to this statement; things are okay but could use tweaking.

☐ GREEN

This statement does not explain my situation; this area is a strength for us, and already working amazing.

5 YOUR CULTURE IS NOT DRIVING THE RIGHT PERFORMANCE.

WHAT THIS MEANS

Misalignment, dysfunction or other cultural or behavioral issues are impacting business performance, employee retention, or brand reputation.

WHY IT MATTERS

Toxic culture = bad business. This also introduces unknowns and integration risks post-acquisition, which can be a major red flag for sophisticated investors & PE firms.

WHAT YOU CAN DO ABOUT IT

- Define, codify and communicate (and often evolve) your business values.
- Align hiring, firing, incentives and performance reviews to your values and culture.
- Ensure your leadership team 'lives' the values and understands HR best practice.

SELF ASSESSMENT

The culture in my business needs review and realignment.

☐ **RED**

This statement represents a real problem for us that we need help solving.

☐ **AMBER**

There is some truth to this statement; things are okay but could use tweaking.

☐ **GREEN**

This statement does not explain my situation; this area is a strength for us, and already working amazing.

6 YOUR BUSINESS IS TOO RELIANT ON THE FOUNDER.

WHAT THIS MEANS

Your business is too dependent on the founder IF removing the founder from business operations creates too much execution risk across the key areas of marketing, sales, delivery, etc … impacting overall financial performance.

WHY IT MATTERS

Sophisticated investors want to buy a 'well-oiled machine'. This means people, teams & infrastructure that will thrive when the founder is not significantly involved. The concept here is called 'transfer value' … which simply means an asset that can transfer in ownership to another entity without the business operation skipping a beat.

WHAT YOU CAN DO ABOUT IT

- Recruit key functional leadership/talent across and through the organization.
- Document founder knowledge, networks, and key relationships … ensure these are shared across the leadership team.
- Test the business operation by having the founder go on a 6-week sabbatical.
- Work towards the 'first' exit. *(This is where the founder hires a new CEO to replace them and elevates their position to the company Board. It's defined as the first exit because the founder can enjoy significant freedom from this one shift alone.)*

SELF ASSESSMENT

My business is overly reliant on the founder and cannot operate effectively if they take a significant (+6-week) leave of absence.

☐ RED

This statement represents a real problem for us that we need help solving.

☐ AMBER

There is some truth to this statement; things are okay but could use tweaking.

☐ GREEN

This statement does not explain my situation; this area is a strength for us, and already working amazing.

7 YOUR BUSINESS RELIES ON 1-2 MAIN CHANNELS FOR ACQUIRING CUSTOMERS.

WHAT THIS MEANS

There are no standardized, measurable processes to generate predictable pipeline opportunities and acquire customers at scale, and the business is overly reliant on 1-2 channels, such as referrals, to drive revenue.

WHY IT MATTERS

Not reliably knowing where your next customer will come from is a big 'Achilles Heel'. Businesses with the highest value have multiple customer acquisition channels in place to mitigate this risk, and can accurately predict their financial performance as a result.

WHAT YOU CAN DO ABOUT IT

- Audit lead generation and sales conversion performance in your business.
- Build target customer acquisition models with clear methods of measurement and ROI.
- Launch multiple lead generation/customer acquisition channels. *(The minimum should be 4, depending on your size & market.)*

SELF ASSESSMENT

My customer acquisition is currently siloed, inconsistent and/or unpredictable ... and I don't really know where my next customer will come from.

☐ RED

This statement represents a real problem for us that we need help solving.

☐ AMBER

There is some truth to this statement; things are okay but could use tweaking.

☐ GREEN

This statement does not explain my situation; this area is a strength for us, and already working amazing.

8 YOUR BUSINESS HAS NO RECURRING REVENUE.

WHAT THIS MEANS

Your revenue and business growth relies heavily on winning new business each day, week or month vs. retaining customers on subscription or long-term contracts.

WHY IT MATTERS

Non-recurring revenue necessitates continually making large investments in marketing and customer acquisition just to fill the sales pipeline, which in turn leads to volatile and inefficient growth, and lower profits.

WHAT YOU CAN DO ABOUT IT

- Implement recurring revenue strategies and models in your business. (i.e. subscriptions, bundling, upsell/cross sell, etc)
- Measure and improve customer net retention over time, together with repeat purchase metrics and customer lifetime value (LTV).
- Invest in technology, and customer success & account management teams, to drive retention.

SELF ASSESSMENT

My business lacks substantial recurring revenue streams currently.

☐ RED

This statement represents a real problem for us that we need help solving.

☐ AMBER

There is some truth to this statement; things are okay but could use tweaking.

☐ GREEN

This statement does not explain my situation; this area is a strength for us, and already working amazing.

9 YOUR BUSINESS RELIES ON ONLY A FEW CUSTOMERS DRIVING THE MAJORITY OF REVENUE.

WHAT THIS MEANS

Too much dependence on one or a few customers for the majority of sales and revenue makes your business vulnerable. This is called a customer concentration risk.

WHY IT MATTERS

Losing one or two big customers at any time, but especially post-exit, can deeply undermine an entire business's revenue and financing, and destroy its value. It's a big red flag when this is identified by a sophisticated buyer during due diligence.

WHAT YOU CAN DO ABOUT IT

- Make sure that the majority of your revenue is not coming from a small number of customers. (*Make sure 80%+ of your revenue is NOT coming from just 20% or less of your customer base.*)
- Expand your total number of customers.
- Diversify across markets, customer segments, and product verticals so you have a well diversified business model.

SELF ASSESSMENT

Most of my revenue currently comes from a small number of customers.

☐ **RED**

This statement represents a real problem for us that we need help solving.

☐ **AMBER**

There is some truth to this statement; things are okay but could use tweaking.

☐ **GREEN**

This statement does not explain my situation; this area is a strength for us, and already working amazing.

10 YOUR BUSINESS LACKS DOCUMENTED SYSTEMS AND PROCESSES.

WHAT THIS MEANS

Lack of documented information, workflows, SOPs, automation & infrastructure will not only stop you from effectively scaling your business, but it will also make it very challenging to transfer the business to a new owner.

WHY IT MATTERS

Sophisticated investors & PE firms will judge your business on people *AND* processes. In fact, this area alone makes up at least 30% of the overall valuation. If things are made up on the fly, with ad hoc workflows and tribal knowledge, then your business has a big continuity risk.

WHAT YOU CAN DO ABOUT IT

- Invest in a strong Ops team that can map your customer journey, including workflows from lead to fulfillment.
- Create systems & playbooks around business-critical functions.
- Use technology to automate repetitive tasks.
- Consider an external validation (*such as Six Sigma*) if your business is heavily reliant on multiple, complex processes to deliver outstanding performance.

SELF ASSESSMENT

My systems and processes are not fully understood or documented well.

☐ **RED**

This statement represents a real problem for us that we need help solving.

☐ **AMBER**

There is some truth to this statement; things are okay but could use tweaking.

☐ **GREEN**

This statement does not explain my situation; this area is a strength for us, and already working amazing.

11 YOUR BUSINESS IS NOT TRACKING OR MEASURING PERFORMANCE EFFECTIVELY.

WHAT THIS MEANS

Not rigorously monitoring data and essential KPIs around lead generation, conversion, churn, LTV etc. means an inability to manage the key drivers of value creation.

WHY IT MATTERS

No metrics/monitoring = no way to review, refine and evolve your strategy. Sophisticated investors & PE firms want to see data-driven, objective management decision making aligned with focused execution.

WHAT YOU CAN DO ABOUT IT

- Identify your top 10-15 essential business KPIs. More is not necessarily better.
- Build real-time automated dashboards and monitor these with an intentional cadence (hourly, daily, weekly etc).
- Distribute daily/weekly/monthly/quarterly KPI reports (as needed in your business) and make key decisions from the information.

SELF ASSESSMENT

I lack adequate visibility and reporting into the KPIs that are crucial in managing my business.

☐ RED

This statement represents a real problem for us that we need help solving.

☐ AMBER

There is some truth to this statement; things are okay but could use tweaking.

☐ GREEN

This statement does not explain my situation; this area is a strength for us, and already working amazing.

12 YOUR FINANCIAL ACCOUNTS ARE NOT AUDIT READY.

WHAT THIS MEANS

How you currently present your business financials won't withstand a sophisticated investor's stringent auditing process during due diligence.

WHY IT MATTERS

Financials alone drive at least 40% of a business valuation. Sophisticated investors & PE firms will use poor financials and unclear information to negotiate the sales price down significantly during the due diligence process (this is called a retrade).

WHAT YOU CAN DO ABOUT IT

- Hire a blue chip CFO, or at the very least, a high-quality accounting firm or fractional CFO, to professionalize your finances.
- Implement GAAP accounting with audit focus 12-36 months before considering selling your business.
- Conduct a Quality of Earnings (QofE) report before you sell your business as this will provide even better information to validate a high valuation.

SELF ASSESSMENT

My financial records wouldn't currently withstand investor scrutiny during a due diligence process.

☐ RED

This statement represents a real problem for us that we need help solving.

☐ AMBER

There is some truth to this statement; things are okay but could use tweaking.

☐ GREEN

This statement does not explain my situation; this area is a strength for us, and already working amazing.

13 YOUR BUSINESS HAS NO ESTABLISHED BOARD OR EXTERNAL ADVISORY TEAM IN PLACE.

WHAT THIS MEANS

The presence of a Board or external advisory team provides guidance, governance, strategic advice, and industry expertise to your business. Not having something like this in place presents risk.

WHY IT MATTERS

Sophisticated investors & PE firms value experience as it decreases risk and influences future performance. Furthermore, the first thing a sophisticated buyer is going to do is put a Board in place when they acquire your business so having this in place in advance is a big driver of confidence and value.

WHAT YOU CAN DO ABOUT IT

- Recruit a business advisor or mentor (at the very least) if you don't currently have one.
- Plan to set up a formal Board at least 12 months or more prior to selling your company (the earlier, the better).
- Schedule quarterly advisory/Board meetings and document the minutes and actions from these meetings.

SELF ASSESSMENT

I currently lack a proper Board and/or external advisory structure in my business.

☐ RED

This statement represents a real problem for us that we need help solving.

☐ AMBER

There is some truth to this statement; things are okay but could use tweaking.

☐ GREEN

This statement does not explain my situation; this area is a strength for us, and already working amazing.

14 YOUR BUSINESS HAS SUBSCALE PROFITABILITY TO BE ATTRACTIVE.

WHAT THIS MEANS

Generating less than $3M in annual net profit or EBITDA puts you below the minimum threshold for many sophisticated investors & PE firms to be interested in acquiring your business.

WHY IT MATTERS

$3M+ net profit or EBITDA signals readiness to scale efficiently via more advanced growth strategies such as partnerships, joint ventures and bolt-on acquisitions. It's also worth mentioning that all deals, big and small, are complex, and sophisticated buyers don't waste their time on small deals where the returns are limited, favoring the larger transactions.

WHAT YOU CAN DO ABOUT IT

- Build a focused, strategic plan to achieve $3M+ EBITDA so you can open up your business for acquisition by the capital markets sophisticated buyers.
- Balance organic growth with advanced growth strategies such as partnerships and acquisitions to scale more quickly.

SELF ASSESSMENT

My business generates under $3M net profit or EBITDA currently.

☐ **RED**

This statement represents a real problem for us that we need help solving.

☐ **AMBER**

There is some truth to this statement; things are okay but could use tweaking.

☐ **GREEN**

This statement does not explain my situation; this area is a strength for us, and already working amazing.

15 YOUR BUSINESS IS NOT READY FOR STRATEGIC SCALE.

WHAT THIS MEANS

Your foundations and infrastructure (people, processes, systems etc) can't currently support larger growth and scale initiatives such as M&A or geographic expansion.

WHY IT MATTERS

Private Equity, in particular, deploy 'buy-and-build' M&A strategies when they acquire businesses and will evaluate your business accordingly to ensure it can either grow via acquisition, or integrate into an existing platform.

WHAT YOU CAN DO ABOUT IT

- Learn about the world of M&A and educate yourself on the latest thinking and practices.
- Build a team that includes M&A capability (either internal or external).
- Acquire businesses as part of your growth strategy before exiting.

SELF ASSESSMENT

My capability and infrastructure cannot currently support growth and scale via M&A.

☐ **RED**

This statement represents a real problem for us that we need help solving.

☐ **AMBER**

There is some truth to this statement; things are okay but could use tweaking.

☐ **GREEN**

This statement does not explain my situation; this area is a strength for us, and already working amazing.

WHERE DO YOU GO FROM HERE?

If you scored one or more of these reasons as '**Red**' and/or '**Amber**' in this guide, there is **good news and bad news**.

The bad news is you have some work to do before your business is going to be appealing to sophisticated investors & PE firms. And remember, these sophisticated buyers are involved in over 70% of all high value transactions.

The good news is addressing these gaps serves to expand the value of your business, regardless of your exit plans, and will provide you with a powerful set of options for when the time comes.

IF YOU ARE SERIOUS ABOUT WANTING TO EXIT YOUR BUSINESS IN THE NEXT 3-5 YEARS, OR AT LEAST BUILD A HIGH-VALUE BUSINESS NOW TO GIVE YOURSELF OPTIONS ...

(And you'd like to see how we can help apply our 15+ years of experience and 100+ acquisitions & exits to your situation), consider joining a **no obligation strategy session** with our team.

When you join the session with us, come prepared with your results based on this Blueprint, so we can get an idea of what's working and what's not working for you. This way we can really focus on those things that are really going to move the needle for you in building a high value, exitable business. And, if there is a good fit, we will recommend you into one of our programs, depending on your situation and goals.

In any case, we hope this **Exit For Millions Blueprint™** helped shed some light on areas in your business that you can work on to help you build a high-value, exitable business that sophisticated investors will be happy to acquire... and we look forward to the opportunity to help you on that journey.

ABOUT THE AUTHOR

Nick Bradley is a global authority on building high-value, exit-ready enterprises. Over the last 20+ years, he has advised multinational corporations and Private Equity firms, and executed over 50 acquisitions, 26 exits, with a combined valuation of over $5 billion. He has personally been involved in 3x exits valued at over $1 billion each.

Nick believes that selling your business isn't a "game of chance". With guidance and support, your business can navigate the complexities of markets, scale efficiently, attain business goals that match your vision, and achieve an outstanding exit that reflects the hard work you have invested in your journey. He also believes in leveling the playing field with sophisticated buyers, such as Private Equity firms, ensuring that business owners are equipped with the strategies and tools to not only compete in the fierce world of M&A, but to win the game.

Today, Nick and his team work exclusively with founders and business owners across the globe helping them scale & sell their companies for maximum value.

www.ingramcontent.com/pod-product-compliance
Lightning Source LLC
LaVergne TN
LVHW070819210926
848482LV00005B/293
* 9 7 8 1 0 6 8 2 4 3 9 4 3 *